MW00474817

To My Granddaughter

With Love

Dates

to